BRAIN-BASED

Life Hacks

for kids!

Dear Parents and Teachers,

This book is needed today more than ever before. For children ages 6-17, anxiety and depression have increased over time (Center for Disease Control). We hope you use this book to have conversations with your kids about how to implement Brain-Based Life Hacks into their lives. Our goal is to empower kids to understand how they can play a more proactive role in their mental health and well-being.

For more information about our program, products, and tools please visit our website: www.MySocialEdge.com

PAGE 1

YOUR NEURONS: Help kids understand the basic parts of a neuron and the function of their neurons. Explain how we are all born with neurons and that during childhood our experiences help form connections to make neuropathways. The more experiences we have, the more neuropathways are formed. The saying goes: *"Neurons that fire together, wire together."* During childhood, the primary job of the brain is to fire neurons and create pathways. During adolescence, the main job of the brain is to become more efficient by focusing on paving (building stronger connections) or pruning (getting rid of the connections that are not in use). We don't need all the neurons we were born with (approximately 100 billion!), so paving focuses on strengthening and making more efficient the connections that are being used while pruning focuses on getting rid of connections that are not being used. During adulthood, we have neuroplasticity. Neuroplasticity is the brain's ability to change and grow throughout a person's life. That's why it's important to continue to learn and experience new things. Help your kids draw out the analogy of a plug being plugged into a socket as you discuss the basic parts of a neuron. If you or your kids are interested in learning more about the brain, we highly recommend the Pathways to Empower program.

PAGES 2-3

YOUR HAPPINESS CHEMICALS: Explain why it's important to lead a balanced life and how this can lead your kids to activating their happiness chemicals. Just as we lead a physically balanced life, it's also important to lead a mentally balanced life. See Dan Siegel's Healthy Mind Platter for more information on this. This book will provide kids with an overview of different ways that they can activate their own happiness chemicals. Talk to them about ways in which they have activated these in the past and even ways they can activate these in their lives today.

PAGE 4

SECRET KINDNESS AGENTS: The concept of Secret Kindness Agents (S.K.A.) was developed by Dr. Ferial Pearson. It is based on the book *Secret Kindness Agents: How Small Acts of Kindness Really Can Change the World.* Have students choose a fun anonymous S.K.A. name (e.g., Chocolate Chip Cookie, aka Triple C) and have them think about small acts of kindness that they can do. The acts of kindness should come from them! 

Positive affirmation cards are definitely a fun way to get started! Talk to your kids about the "helper's high" and how kindness is not only good for others – but also good for them!

Please note: For educators, Dr. Ferial Pearson also came out with an educator's guide that discusses how educational professionals have implemented the Secret Kindness Agent project from preschool through university levels.

PAGE 5

SELF-COMPASSION: Show kids the self-compassion comic and have them brainstorm a comic for themselves. On a separate piece of paper or a whiteboard, have them draw out a comic of a mistake they often make. Discuss with kids how they feel after making that particular mistake. What do they typically say to themselves? Are they harder on themselves than they are on others? Why do you think this is the case?

Next, discuss the **three main tenets** of self-compassion:
1. **Self-Kindness.** Be kind to yourself like you would to a friend. What would a good friend say?
2. **Common Humanity.** Talk about how everyone in the world makes mistakes and that's what connects us to one another.
3. **Mindfulness.** Stay in the present moment versus thinking about the past. Ask kids what strategies they currently use for staying in the present. Discuss mindfulness strategies they can use such as Mindfulness 5-4-3-2-1. With this strategy, kids acknowledge 5 things they can see, 4 things they can touch, 3 things they can hear, 2 things they can smell, and 1 thing they can taste.

PAGE 6

INNER CRITIC: Have kids close their eyes and imagine their "judge/inner critic." This is the voice that is their harshest critic! Next, have them imagine their "powerful ally/inner nurturer." This is the voice that is their superhero. It lifts them up when they are down and protects them! Next, have them write down their mistakes or insecurities. Have them cross each one off the list and talk back to their judge/inner critic. For example, kids can say *"You lie. I'm not listening to you anymore. Go away!"* Then have kids think about what their inner nurturer would say instead. Have them create a positive affirmation and think about activities that go along with it to get their mind off the mistake or insecurity.

PAGE 7

THE POWER OF NO: Have kids take the introvert/extrovert quiz and discuss the ways in which they can get energy from people or have their energy drained from people. Talk to kids about times when they have wanted to say "no" to others but found that it was difficult for them to do so. Discuss how saying no to others means saying yes to oneself.

PAGE 8

HOW DO YOU WANT TO SPEND YOUR TIME?
Encourage kids to think about how they want to spend their time. The more they know about themselves and what they like or dislike, the easier it will be for them to make the decision to say "no" or "yes."

PAGE 9 — **"NO" IS OFTEN THE HARDEST WORD TO SAY!** Who is it easy to say no to? (e.g., family) Who is more difficult to say no to? (e.g., certain friends). Remind kids that when they say "no" to something they don't want to do, they are actually saying "yes." Role-play different ways they can say no next time. Use the strategy **S.T.O.P.** Research shows role-playing is an active learning strategy that promotes self-reflection and awareness.

PAGE 10-11 — **AUTHENTIC FRIENDSHIPS:** Talk to kids about how they evaluate friendships. What are characteristics they are looking for in the good friends? Discuss what it means to have a green light, yellow light, or red light friend. Have kids discuss what would put a friend in one of those categories. Discuss what their core values are. Core values are guiding principles that help individuals differentiate between what is right or wrong. Do their friends share their values, such as kindness and compassion? Have them think through each prompt. When kids think about their friendships, considering their core values can help them determine which friendships are authentic.

PAGE 12 — **CONFLICT RESOLUTION SKILLS:** Discuss what kids do with their yellow or red light friends. Discuss key tenets of conflict resolution with the acronym: *The Ostrich Feels Naïve*. Help them understand that there are strategies that can help them resolve conflicts without it turning into drama or a major blow-up. Role-play situations in which kids wait for the right timing, state their observations, discuss their feelings and address their needs. This will help them be ready for the next time they want to use this strategy in their lives.

PAGE 13 — **DOPAMINE, THE REWARD CENTER: Peer Pressure.** First, discuss how a brain responds to peer pressure. This is why peer pressure often works and why it's important to distinguish between positive and negative peer pressure. Kids can use positive peer pressure to their benefit and reach their goals. It's important to assess times when they have been under negative peer pressure and to discuss what strategies can be used so that they can think clearly about the decisions they want to make. Remind students to walk away from peers (if possible), use the strategy **S.T.O.P.** (p.9), and think about whether or not they really want to engage in the activity.

PAGE 14 — **DIFFERENT TYPES OF NEGATIVE PEER PRESSURE:** Explore the different types of negative peer pressure. Once kids can label the peer pressure, they will know that it is negative and they will be able to think through what they want to do. Ask them if they have encountered any of these situations in their lives. Discuss the situations that may not have come up yet. Research shows that it is best to deal with peer pressure before it happens. Help kids think through strategies on how to deal with each scenario if they arise.

Discuss why explanations like "everyone is doing it" are not really a reason to engage in the same activity. Similarly, when popular kids all start wearing particular brands or have the latest gadgets, have kids think about whether they really want the item or whether they only want it because other kids have it. Discuss how they would feel if someone was putting them down, rejecting them, giving them the look, or huddling together to leave them out. Help kids become upstanders for other kids who are being pressured to do something they don't want to do.

PAGE 15-16

DOPAMINE LOOPS: Help kids understand when they are in a dopamine loop. Many kids don't really realize the ways that social media or gaming can keep them in a dopamine loop. Being in a dopamine loop keeps them from achieving other goals, because they are being instantly gratified. Remind them that the more experiences they have, the more they are building neuropathways. It's important to have a wide range of experiences and to live a balanced life from optimal brain chemistry. Have kids write out more stop/counter movements they can do when they are in a dopamine loop. Discuss the listed dopamine loop activities and non-dopamine loop activities, then have kids add more next to the check marks provided.

PAGE 17-19

DOPAMINE & RISKY BEHAVIOR: Take Good Risks, Be an Active Creator. Try the Cortex College Consulting Formula: Encourage kids to be active creators by launching their own unique project! This allows them to feel good about themselves and develop their abilities. It also builds their self-efficacy. Help kids take good risks. Encourage them to grow by putting their work, their abilities, and their passions out into the world! **Cortex College Consulting** helps students develop their passions using a unique, specialized formula for coming up with project ideas. With this formula, kids are encouraged to think about their abilities, their skills, and areas that might provide some discomfort to them. They will learn that a growth mindset involves stepping out of their comfort zone in order to grow their mind, abilities, and skills in new ways. Using this method, kids will come up with tangible project ideas they can launch to make an impact in the world. Brainstorm with kids using the exercise on p.18. Have them come up with three project ideas and present their ideas to family members or friends. Then, help them pick one idea that they can work on as their passion project!

PAGE 20

DOPAMINE, THE REWARD CENTER: Achieve Your Goals. Research shows that when you can visualize yourself doing something, it is more likely to happen. Have kids be as specific as possible when they are thinking about their goals with the power of the three Ws: *What will they do? When will they do it? Where will they do it?* Have them visualize transitioning from one activity to the next. Connect specific tasks to their passion project from p.19. Oftentimes, when a project requires a lot of attention it can seem daunting, so help kids break their passion project into more manageable tasks. Then use the three Ws to help kids come up with an action plan for completing the tasks.

Kids may need more than four tasks to complete their passion project. Assure them that's OK. Have them use another journal to brainstorm more Passion Project tasks to complete their passion project. The more tasks kids check off, the more they activate their dopamine by checking tasks off their list!

PAGE 21

TEMPTATION BUNDLING TO ACHIEVE GOALS: Discuss how kids can use temptation bundling to achieve their goals and activate dopamine and serotonin. The key here is that we can combine instant and delayed gratification to reach our goals! **Note:** It's important to remember why kids are pursuing the goal. Have them think about their passion project and the tasks that they have broken down to complete it. Also, have them think about other goals that would get them out of their comfort zone (use pp.17-18). Have them connect it with something that they want to do right now (instant gratification) but remind them they can only do it after completing their goal and at no other time in the day. That's how the magic of temptation bundling works!

PAGE 22

THE SECRET TO HAPPINESS IS GRATEFULNESS: There is a significant amount of research on gratitude. Gratitude has been linked to better mental health, better relationships, and a sense of fulfillment. Gratitude lowers levels of stress, reduces anxious thoughts, and helps individuals get better sleep. Not only are people happier, but they are also healthier!

PAGE 23

MY GRATITUDE JOURNAL: Remind kids that they can't focus on positive and negative thoughts at the same time. When they are focusing on positive thoughts, they can't also focus on negative thoughts. Practicing gratitude allows them to cultivate an "attitude of gratitude." The more we practice it, the better our neurons get at looking for it. With practice, the brain starts looking for more things to be grateful for. Encourage kids to keep a gratefulness journal by their beds. Before going to bed, they should write three things they are grateful for. Research shows that focusing on things that you are grateful for will help you sleep better. Doing this right before bed replaces anxiety and worrying with positive thinking. This, in turn, allows for them to sleep better at night.

PAGE 24

CO-CREATING A CONTRACT: As kids get older, they want to have power and control over their lives. Parents still need to guide their children, however, because the adolescent brain is still developing. Kids should know that the prefrontal cortex – which is responsible for organizing, planning, and thinking through decisions – will not be fully formed until they reach 25 years of age. Co-creating contracts allows for parents and their kids to come to a mutual agreement. Together, think through the goals that are important for your child, and help them balance working on their goals (delayed gratification) with the things they want to do in the moment (instant gratification). This will help them lead a more balanced life, and it will help build important neuropathways!

Sincerely,

Amita Roy Shah, Ed.D.

SOCIAL EDGE©

YOUR NEURONS

A neuron, or nerve cell, helps you process and interact with the world. As you make sense of the world, these specialized cells create electrical impulses in the brain. There is an average of *100 billion neurons* in the brain.

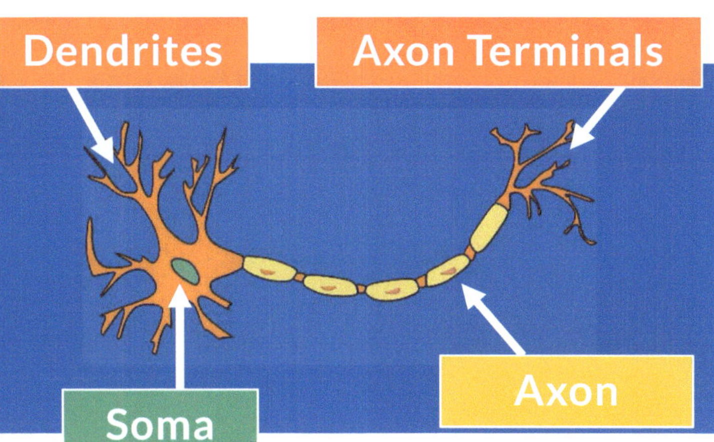

Each neuron has an **axon** that sends signals and **dendrites** that receive signals. The axons are *activated* when neurons want to talk to other neurons. Neurons send an electrical message called an **action potential** through their **axon terminal**, and the action potential causes the release of **neurotransmitters**. The dendrites receive the messages sent from the axons of other neurons.

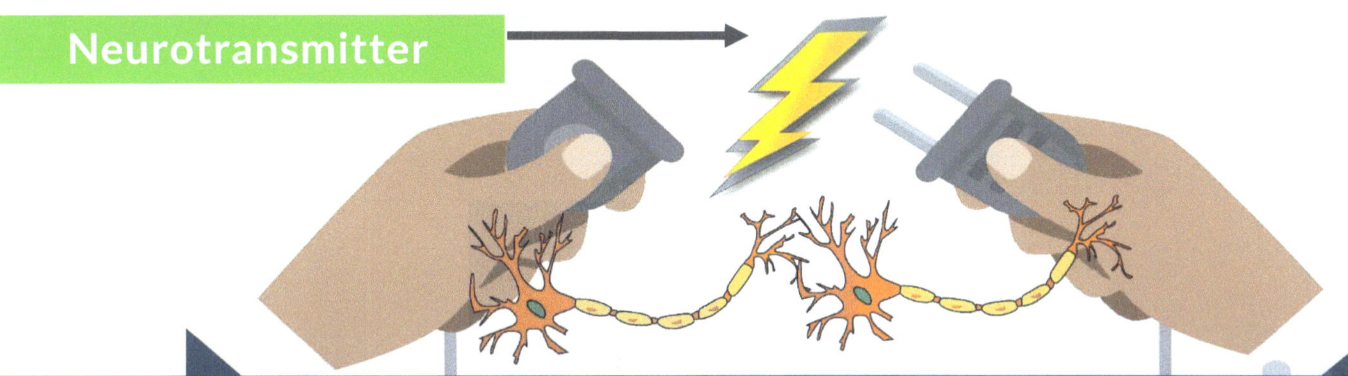

When you want to light a lamp, you can activate it by grabbing the plug. You plug the cord (axon, sends signals) into a socket (dendrite, receives signals), and the light bulb (neurotransmitter) is activated!

Activate the light bulb, or your neurotransmitters, by drawing a picture of a cord (axon) that is getting plugged into a socket (dendrite). Draw the light bulb too. Label the pictures: axon, dendrite, neurotransmitter.

YOUR HAPPINESS
Chemicals

NEUROTRANSMITTERS are chemical messengers. They are activated by the **axon** and received by the **dendrite**. There are four chemicals in your body that are known as happiness chemicals: oxytocin, serotonin, dopamine, and endorphins. Happiness chemicals are neurotransmitters. Just like grabbing a plug, you can activate your happiness chemicals!

DENDRITE
(receiving signals)

AXON
(sending signals)

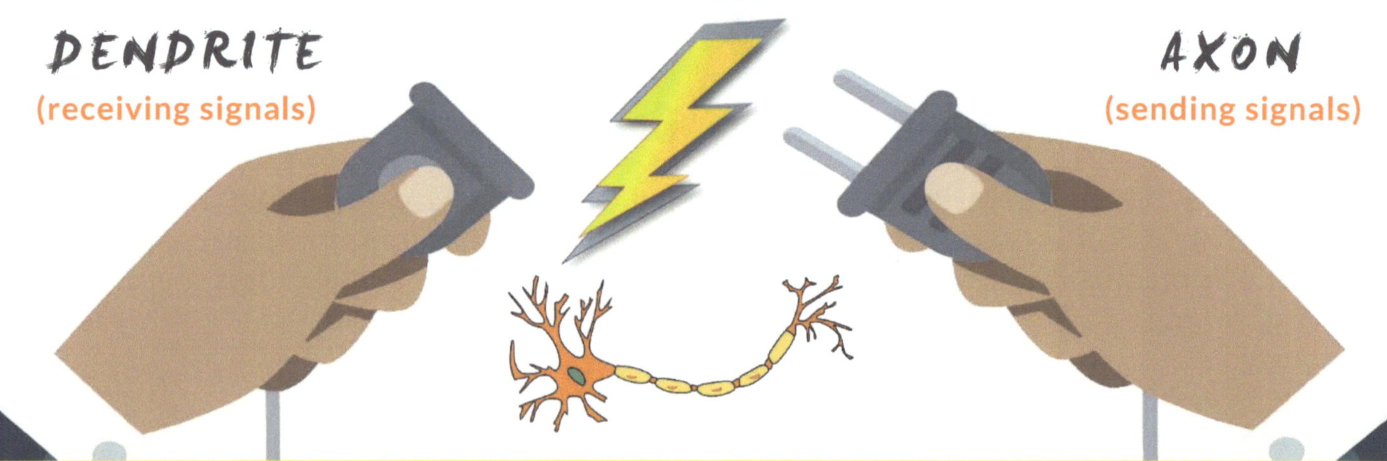

Happiness hacks are ways you can activate your happiness chemicals:

OXYTOCIN

This is known as the "love" hormone because it plays a role in social bonds. You can increase oxytocin by spending time with family and friends.

SEROTONIN

This regulates your mood. You can increase serotonin through exposure to sunlight, meditating, having a positive mindset, or practicing gratitude. Serotonin brings about feelings of confidence and self-esteem.

DOPAMINE

This is known for helping with motivation and achievement. Dopamine pushes you to get stuff done. It is also linked to the pleasure and reward system of your brain.

ENDORPHINS

This is a natural painkiller. Your body releases endorphins in response to stress or pain. For example, endorphins can be released when you run, sometimes causing what is known as a "runner's high." And endorphins can be released when you laugh. Yes, laughter therapy is a real thing!

UNDERSTANDING YOUR
Happiness Chemicals

Write in the name of **one happiness chemical** that goes with each situation, then **draw the emoticon** that represents each happiness chemical.

 = oxytocin　 = serotonin　 = dopamine　PAIN = endorphins

	You Most Likely Activate This When...	Your Happiness Chemical	Draw the Emoticon
1	...you hang out with good friends after school.		
2	...you watch a comedy show and can't stop laughing!		
3	...you sit on a bench to get some sunlight.		
4	...you get an A on your science test.		
5	...you get a hug from a parent.		
6	...you go for a run when you wake up.		
7	...you meditate for 5 minutes every day.		
8	...you check off a task from your to-do list.		
9	...you go to a party and make new friends.		
10	...you write down something you are grateful for each night.		

DID YOU KNOW?

Your happiness chemicals can be activated when you eat a balanced meal, exercise, get enough sleep, meditate, spend time with good friends, laugh often, practice gratitude, and work towards your goals!

*NOTE: More than one can apply. To get familiar with the happiness chemicals, pick one based on the information from p.2.

ANSWERS: 1) O 2) E 3) S 4) D 5) O 6) E 7) S 8) D 9) O 10) S

Secret Kindness Agents

SECRET STRATEGY #1:

BE KIND

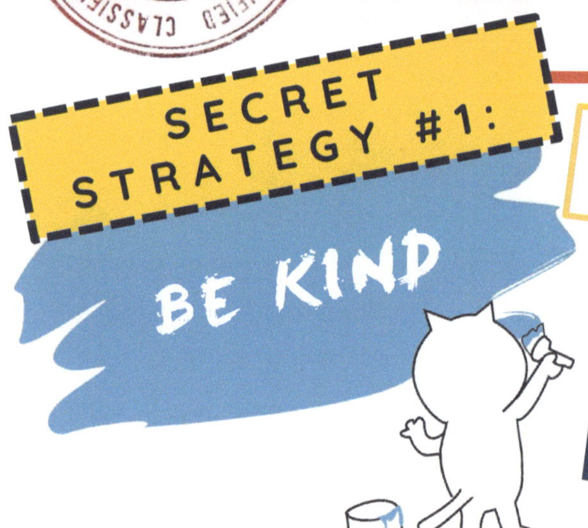

Secret Kindness Agents* (S.K.A.) are happier, they are healthier, and they can change the world!

DID YOU KNOW?

Kindness boosts your oxytocin, serotonin, and dopamine levels! It also causes your body to give off endorphins, letting you experience a "helper's high."

Create an S.K.A. Name

How does being kind help you?

____

____

____

Who and what inspires you to be kind?

____

____

____

List five ways to be kind:

1 ________________________________

2 ________________________________

3 ________________________________

4 ________________________________

5 ________________________________

#RAKE

Do Random Acts of Kindness Everywhere (#RAKE). Create a positive affirmation card, then hand it to someone or leave it on someone's car or doorstep. Remember to sign your S.K.A. name on the card!

Some examples of positive affirmations to get you started on those cards: *You are capable of amazing things! You got this! Anything can happen in one day. Believe in the magic of today and believe in yourself! Sending you positive vibes today! Follow your dreams, work hard, make it happen!*

By doing this one act, you might inspire someone else to do the same.

 **Kindness is contagious!**

When you are feeling down, remember that doing one act of kindness a day can activate your neurotransmitters.

***Concept by Dr. Ferial Pearson**

Self-Compassion

You should treat yourself with the same kindness, concern, and support you would show a friend.
By treating yourself like a friend, you will be happier and you will be able to bounce back from your mistakes faster to achieve what you set out to do!

What is Self-Compassion?

1 — Self-Kindness
Stop being so critical of yourself. Treat and talk to yourself as you would a good friend.

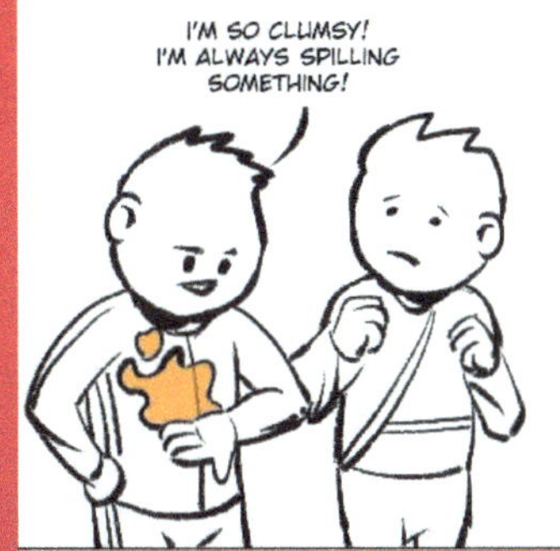

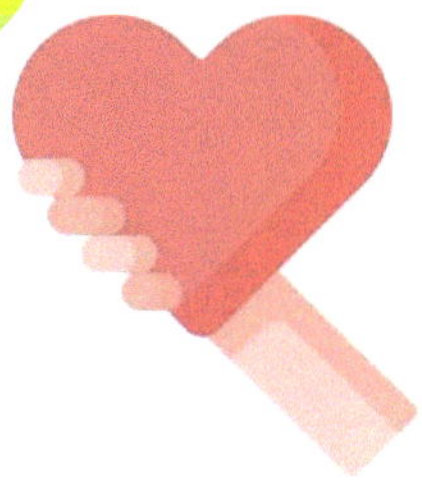

2 — Common Humanity
We are all imperfect and this is a shared human experience. Connect with others – you're not alone.

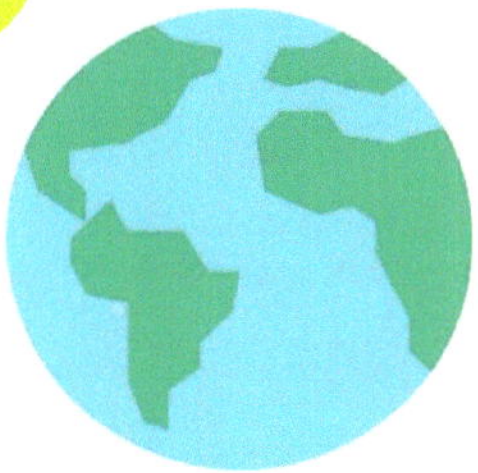

3 — Mindfulness
Be open to the reality of the present moment. Acknowledge how you feel without exaggeration.

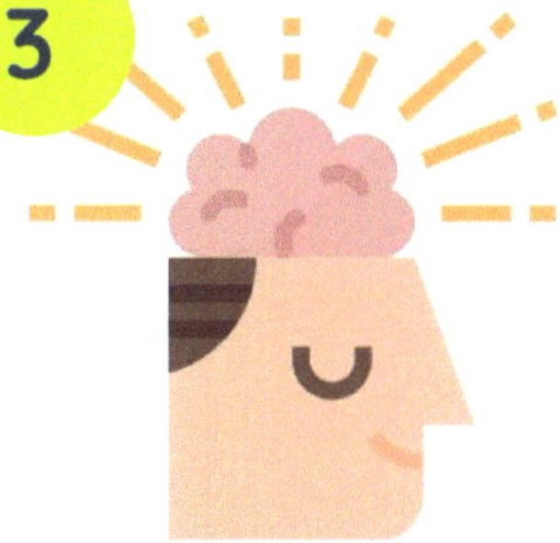

"YOU ARE AWESOME!" "YOU ROCK!" "YOU ARE BRAVE!"

The Inner Critic

We all have an inner critic.

Your inner critic is your inner voice that may be criticizing and judging you. We will call it your judge. We also have an inner nurturer that lifts you up and protects you! Your inner nurturer is your most powerful ally.

Draw a picture of "judge/inner critic"	Draw a picture of "powerful ally/inner nurturer"

Mistakes/insecurities: *"I always..."*	**What would you say to a good friend who has the same problem as you?**	**Use a positive affirmation:** *"I am...awesome, kind, brave."* Also, think of a fun activity to go with it, like yoga or shooting hoops.

1. **Cross out all your mistakes/insecurities** from the list above.
2. **Get control of your "judge/inner critic"** by not listening and/or talking back to it.
3. **Try using one of your activity ideas** alongside a positive affirmation. In addition to yoga or shooting hoops, other examples include running, swimming, squeezing a stress ball, playing/listening to music, or meditating.

The Power of No

The power of no means saying "yes" to yourself and activating your happiness chemicals: serotonin and dopamine.

When somebody asks you to do something, how do you respond?
While you may often want to please the person asking, you should ask yourself whether what they are asking for is something you actually want to do… or would you rather be doing something else? Oftentimes, we put others' needs before our own!

For each of the questions below, decide whether A or B describes you better.
CIRCLE YOUR ANSWER.

1
 A. Do you feel energized after being around people?
 B. Do you feel tired after being around people?

2
 A. Do you have many friends?
 B. Do you have a few, close friends?

3
 A. Do you prefer talking with someone rather than sitting alone?
 B. Do you prefer spending time alone rather than being with people all the time?

4
 A. Do you express yourself better with your words?
 B. Do you express yourself better in writing?

5
 A. Do you seem like you are always out and about and "*on the go*"?
 B. Do you like taking your time to think about things before you do them?

YOUR RESULTS

If you answered A for most questions, you are an extrovert. Extroverts get their energy from social situations. They tend to be vocal about their preferences and choices. They aren't likely to dwell on problems or difficulties. They generally enjoy talking to people rather than being alone, and they often make new friends easily.

If you answered B for most questions, you are an introvert. Introverts can get drained from social situations. They generally get their energy from spending time alone. They are often self-aware and spend time focusing on their inner thoughts, feelings, or moods. Introverts likely have a small group of close friends.

If you answered A or B pretty equally, you are an ambivert. An ambivert is a person whose personality has a balance of extrovert and introvert characteristics.

SOCIAL EDGE©

How Do You Want to Spend Your Time?

Check the boxes that you believe represent you or what you like to do. Put a question mark next to any boxes you aren't sure about. Mark an "X" in any box that definitely doesn't represent you.

START HERE!

	Friends		Experimenting		Sports
	Family		Robotics/Technology		Being in Nature
	Hobbies		After-School Clubs		Learning Something New
	TV/Movies		Creating Products		Sleeping
	Social Media		Cooking/Baking		Reading
	Art		Gaming		Engineering
	Singing		Running		Dining/Eating
	Dancing		Biking		Animating
	Organization		Arts & Crafts		Playing an Instrument
	Podcasts		Performing		Listening to Music

1 What do you typically spend your time doing?

____

____

2 What do you wish you had more time to do?

____

____

3 What do you wish you could say no to sometimes?

____

____

____

____

"NO" is often the hardest word to say!

So what are some strategies that can help?

Use the strategy S.T.O.P.

S → **Stop** and check in with yourself about the decision.

T → **Take** a deep breath. Do a mind and body scan.

O → **Observe** your thoughts and feelings about the situation. What are your needs right now? Are you feeling tired or overwhelmed? Will saying "yes" add more stress to you? Would you rather be doing something else with your time?

P → **Proceed**. Make a decision. Yes or no.

If your answer is a no, say no in a polite way.

✓ *Thanks for thinking of me, but I'm just exhausted today and need some downtime.*

✓ *That will not work for me today, but maybe next time.*

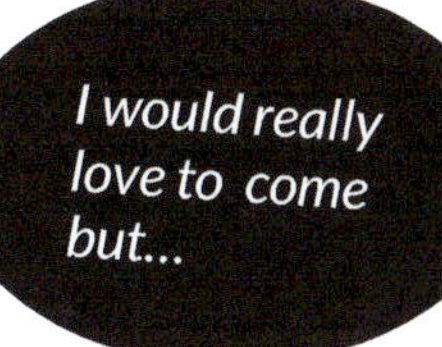

Write out 3 more ways you can say no:

1 ______________________________

____

2 ______________________________

____

3 ______________________________

____

Authentic Friendships

SECRET STRATEGY #4:

Having authentic friends boosts your *oxytocin* and *serotonin*!

What are some characteristics of good friends?

How do you evaluate friendships?

Evaluate each of these statements by coloring in the green, yellow, or red light.

Green = Go → *You feel safe. You can trust your friend. You know this friend cares about you.*
Yellow = Use Caution → *Sometimes you don't feel safe. Sometimes, you feel like you can't trust them.*
Red = Stop → *Often makes you feel unsafe. You often feel criticized or used by them.*

	STATEMENTS	STOP LIGHT
1	Your friend always makes the plans.	
2	Your friend laughs at you when you are hurt or in trouble.	
3	Your friend helps you when you are really in trouble.	
4	Your friend is funny and fun to be around.	
5	Your friend sometimes criticizes the way you dress or look.	
6	Your friend borrows money and doesn't pay you back.	
7	Your friend gets irritated with you sometimes and tells you to give him/her space.	
8	Your friend takes into consideration what you want to do.	
9	Your friend remembers special days, like your birthday.	
10	Your friend asks if you need help when they see you struggling with something.	

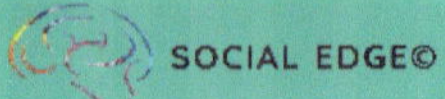

STATEMENTS (continued)	STOP LIGHT
11 Your friend is fun to be around and you feel safe with them.	
12 Your friend is moody and you are not sure if they will be nice or mean to you when you meet with them.	
13 Your friend likes you because you have nice things.	
14 Your friend hangs out with you because you are friends with someone else that they want to get to know.	
15 Your friend is always there for you and checks in on you.	
16 Your friend needs you to text them back right away.	
17 Your friend will talk to you at school, but won't spend time with you outside of school or online (e.g., texting).	
18 Your friend thinks they are right all the time and won't take your perspective into consideration.	
19 Your friend only calls when they want something.	
20 Your friend puts you down or makes fun of you in front of others.	
21 You feel bad about yourself after you've spent time with your friend.	
22 Your friend is accepting of who you are and doesn't try to change you.	
23 Your friend is a good listener.	
24 Your friend is not happy for you when good things happen.	
25 Your friend brings drama into your life.	
26 Your friend complains about you behind your back.	
27 Your friend bails on you at the last minute.	
28 Your friend uses your secrets against you and shares them.	
29 Your friend is a bad influence and makes you do things that get you into trouble.	
30 Your friend excludes you from things with mutual friends.	

We will never find the perfect friend, but once we begin to become aware of our own needs and wants then we can know what's important to us and what's not! It's important to find friends who share our core values.

STOP AND THINK!
What should you do with your yellow light or red light friends: distance, discuss, or something else?

SOCIAL EDGE©

Conflict Resolution Skills

Don't fall into the OSTRICH TRAP!

The idea that ostriches bury their heads in the sand when faced with a dangerous or uncomfortable situation is a myth! Ostriches don't really bury their heads in the sand to make them invisible to predators. 😆

The real reason ostriches put their heads in the ground is because that's where they lay their eggs. Ostriches might look like they are hiding when they bury their heads in the sand, but they are actually just checking on their eggs.

Still, you don't want to fall into the mythical ostrich trap of avoiding uncomfortable situations! Don't just run away or hide from conflict; this will cause you to procrastinate and not address the real issue. Instead, there are specific strategies you can use to resolve your problems.

Remember the Ostrich Trap: "The Ostrich Feels Naïve!"
"The Ostrich Feels Naïve" is an acronym that can help you decide what to do when you're in conflict with a friend.

Timing matters. When you are calm and in a place free of distractions, make time to really talk.

Observations. State what you have observed without any judgment. This is hard and takes some practice.

Feelings. Connect to feelings. Try saying, *"I feel _____________ when _________ happens."* Remember, how you say it matters! There is a difference between assertive and aggressive communication styles.

Needs and next steps. Come to a mutual understanding about what your needs are and what the next steps should be.

Peer Pressure

SECRET STRATEGY #5:

This Is Your Brain on Peer Pressure

Dopamine is released when your brain expects a reward. When you are with friends, and your friends tell you to do something, dopamine anticipates being rewarded with smiles, compliments, or high fives from them. When dopamine is released, it will want you to "just do it." Know the difference between positive and negative peer pressure.

Dopamine gives off more signals saying *"Just do it!"* when you are with your friends than when you are alone!

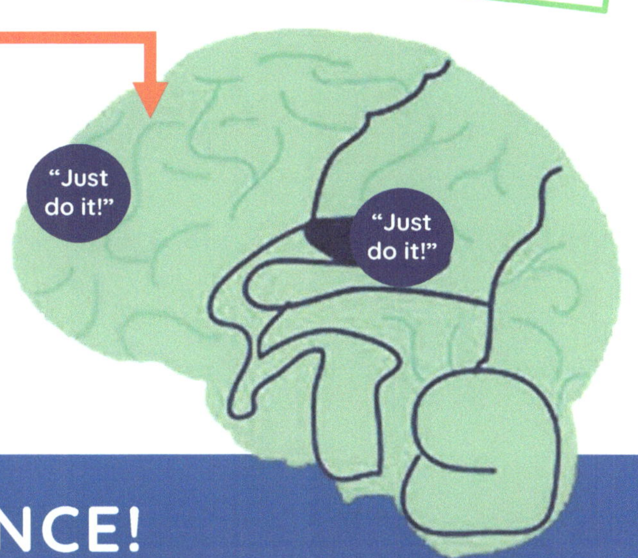

KNOW THE DIFFERENCE!

What is positive peer pressure?

positive influence on life goals (e.g., when you improve your grades or exercise)

What is negative peer pressure?

negative influence on life goals (e.g., when you adopt dangerous or risky habits)

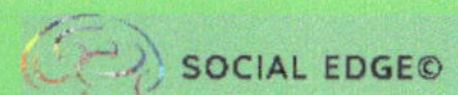

Different Types of Negative

Peer Pressure

In each box below, **draw a picture** and **write a few words** that provide an example of verbal and nonverbal forms of peer pressure. Think about times you have been in these types of situations and what you said or did.

Verbal	Nonverbal
Reasoning: giving reasons for why something is OK to do *(e.g., cheating)*	**The Look:** kids who give a "look" that says "we are cool, and you are not" *(e.g., school dance)*
Put-Downs: insulting or calling someone names to make them feel bad *(e.g., being called a loser)*	**The Popular:** popular kids buy or wear something as an example for others to follow *(e.g, brand names)*
Rejection: threatening to leave someone out or end a friendship *(e.g., not being invited to a party)*	**The Huddle:** a group that huddles together and doesn't let an individual into the huddle to see or hear what they are doing *(e.g., watching a YouTube video)*

Dopamine Loops
The Good, the Bad, and the Ugly

SECRET STRATEGY #6:

Dopamine can work towards or against your life goals. *Notice when you are in a dopamine loop and use countermovements to stop!*

What happens in a dopamine loop?

Dopamine anticipates a reward when it sees something pleasurable like your phone → it gets the **reward** (likes, notifications, scrolling) → it keeps searching for the **next reward.**

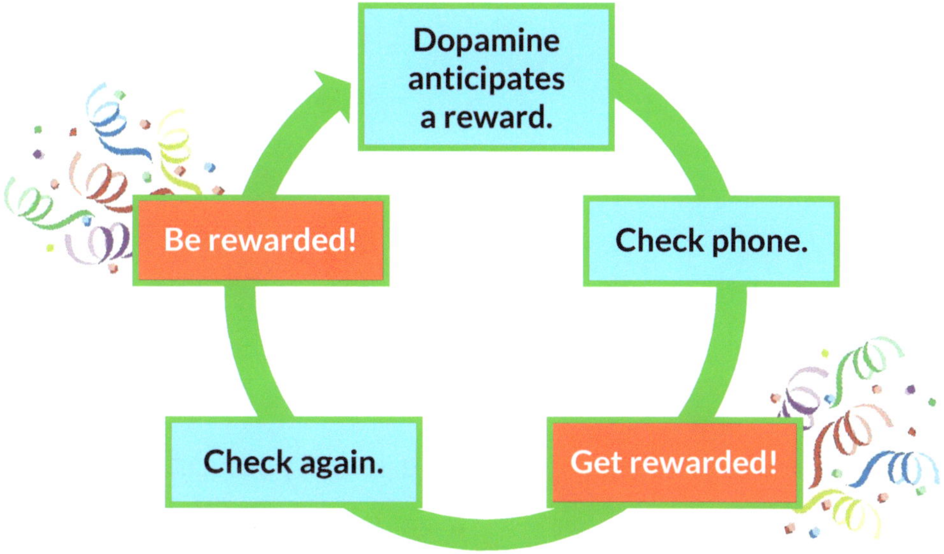

How can you get out of a dopamine loop?

A countermovement is one way to get out of the dopamine loop. It's a physical movement that will become a conditioned response every time you do it. **Here are some stop/countermovements:**

- ✓ Push the home button.
- ✓ Put it down/shut it off.
- ✓ Move away from the object.
- ✓ Change your environment.
- ✓ Engage in a non-dopamine loop activity.

What are some dopamine loop activities?

- ✓ Some Netflix shows
- ✓ Social media
- ✓ Drugs
- ✓ Vaping/cigarettes
- ✓ Alcohol

- ✓ Sweets/sugar

What are some non-dopamine loop activities?

- ✓ Playing basketball
- ✓ Baking or cooking
- ✓ Playing music

SMART HACK!

Did you know that phones are a brain drain?

Research proves that if you keep your phone next to you when you do school work, you actively spend brain power resisting your phone – even if it is off!

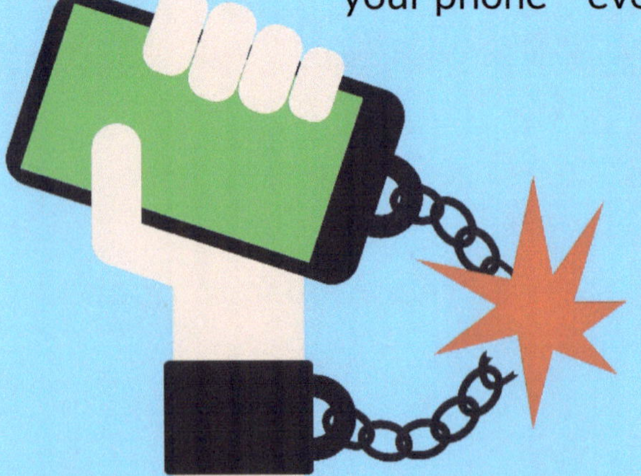

Keep your phone in another room so you can increase your cognitive capacity (your brain's ability to hold and process data) for more important tasks.

Dopamine & Risky Behavior

Take Good Risks, Be an Active Creator

Use dopamine to be an active creator versus a passive consumer. By taking good risks and actively creating something, you will increase your self-confidence.

Dopamine influences your mood and feelings of reward and motivation. Taking good risks allows for you to reach your life goals and be an active creator versus a passive consumer.

Let's figure out how you can take risks and actively create a unique project with **Cortex College Consulting's unique formula:**

Formats + Interests + Skills + Growth = Unique Project Idea

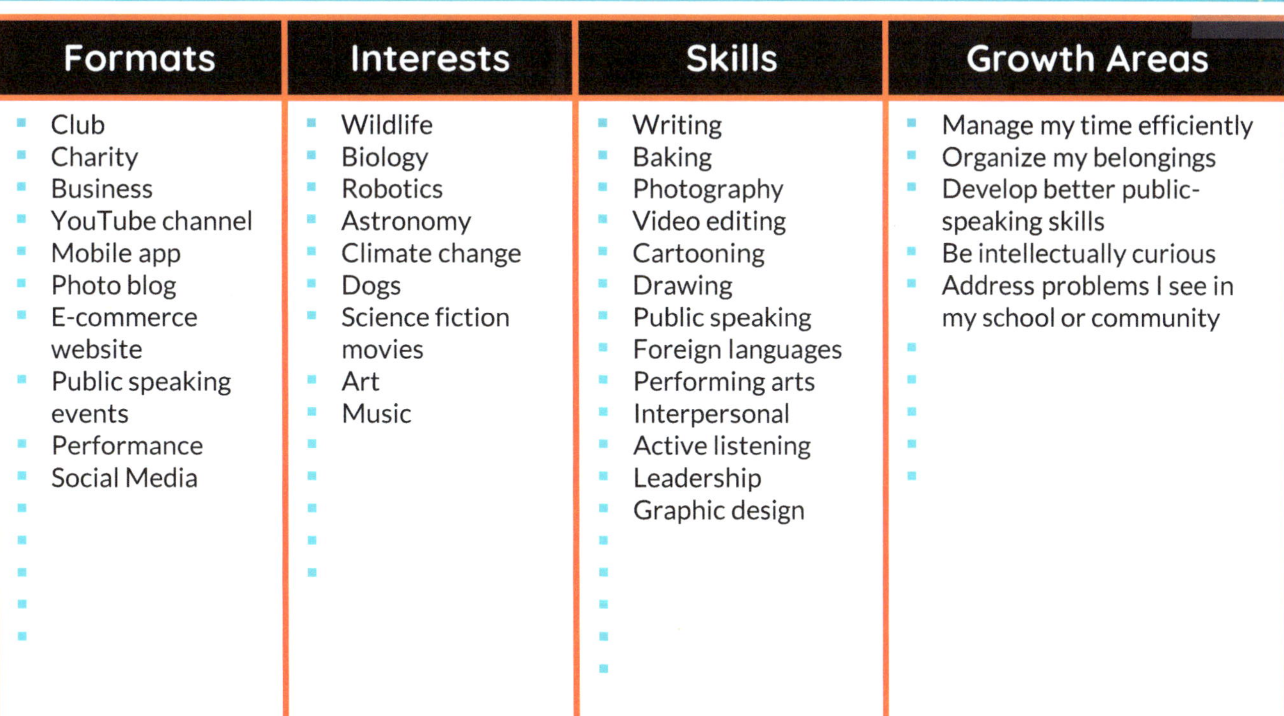

Formats	Interests	Skills	Growth Areas
Club	Wildlife	Writing	Manage my time efficiently
Charity	Biology	Baking	Organize my belongings
Business	Robotics	Photography	Develop better public-speaking skills
YouTube channel	Astronomy	Video editing	Be intellectually curious
Mobile app	Climate change	Cartooning	Address problems I see in my school or community
Photo blog	Dogs	Drawing	
E-commerce website	Science fiction movies	Public speaking	
Public speaking events	Art	Foreign languages	
Performance	Music	Performing arts	
Social Media		Interpersonal	
		Active listening	
		Leadership	
		Graphic design	

Fill out these boxes to learn more about your
formats, interests, skills, and growth areas:

FORMATS

What types of formats do I enjoy working with?

IN-PERSON:
- ❑ Clubs
- ❑ Events
- ❑ Public Speaking
- ❑ Performance
- ❑
- ❑

TECHNOLOGY:
- ❑ Videos
- ❑ Social media
- ❑ Animating
- ❑
- ❑

CREATE:
- ❑ Business
- ❑ Charity
- ❑ Portfolio
- ❑ Writing
- ❑ Newspaper
- ❑ Magazine

- ❑ Blog
- ❑
- ❑
- ❑
- ❑
- ❑

INTERESTS

What are things I like to do outdoors? (e.g. hiking, gardening, tennis)	*What are things I like to do inside my home and why? (e.g., reading, movies)*	*What are my favorite things to do with technology and why? (e.g.,YouTube)*	*What are my favorite activities or hobbies? (e.g., baking)*

SKILLS

What are my hard skills/ strengths? (e.g., writing, software skills, mathematics, task specific)	*What are my favorite subjects in school?*	*What projects do I like to work on when I'm not in school? (e.g., scrapbooking)*	*What are my best soft skills? (e.g., active listener, communicator, making decisions, creative, etc.)*

GROWTH AREAS

What skills am I interested in learning more about?	*What types of social change am I passionate about? (e.g., cyberbullying, kindness, conserving water)*	*What types of problems do I see in my school or community? (e.g., racism, screens, anxiety)*	*What is an area of weakness that I want to get better at? (e.g., time management, public speaking)*

Use the Cortex College Consulting formula above to come up with three project ideas. Each project idea is created by combining one item from each of the four columns. Then, rank your ideas from favorite to least favorite and write 2-3 sentences about why your favorite idea landed on top. Ask for feedback from a friend, sibling, or parent to see what they think of the idea and to determine how feasible it would be for you to work on the idea.

For example,

1 **Create a new Instagram account** [format] showcasing your cartoons [interest] based on your cartooning skills [skills], and challenge yourself to create political cartoons about current events [growth area].

2 **Create a community organization** [format] by starting a community garden [interest] using your gardening and leadership skills [skills], and challenge yourself to approach community members you don't know to help with creating the community garden [growth area].

3 **Create a series of social events** [format] to debate controversial topics [interests] using your public speaking skills [skills], and challenge yourself to market the event using social media and technology to create newsletters and flyers [growth area].

Now, Your Turn...

1 Create

2 Create

3 Create

Achieve Your Goals ✓

SECRET STRATEGY #8:

Use the "three Ws" to visualize your intention. *This will help you achieve your goals and activate your dopamine by checking it off!*

The goals that are important are usually not as urgent or as fun as your temptations!

THE THREE Ws → What? When? Where?

I will [research how to start a blog] at [6pm] in my [bedroom on my desk].

Take a look at **Secret Strategy #7:** What do you want to actively create?

Break it down into smaller tasks. For each task, write in **the three Ws** and visualize it happening!

What will you create?
This is your passion project.

TASK 1

What? ______________________
When? ______________________
Where? ______________________

TASK 2

What? ______________________
When? ______________________
Where? ______________________

TASK 3

What? ______________________
When? ______________________
Where? ______________________

TASK 4

What? ______________________
When? ______________________
Where? ______________________

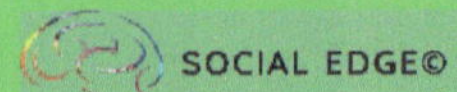

Use Temptation Bundling*

To Achieve Goals 

SECRET STRATEGY #9:

Use temptation bundling to achieve your goals and activate *dopamine* and *serotonin*!

Temptation bundling can boost your willpower! It is getting to do something you really want (*instant gratification*), right after you achieve one of your goals (*delayed gratification*)!

Note: *You can only act on the temptation after achieving a task from your list of goals, and at no other time in the day!*

Write down some of your goals here. Remember to think about the new skills or growth areas you explored with **Secret Strategy #7.**

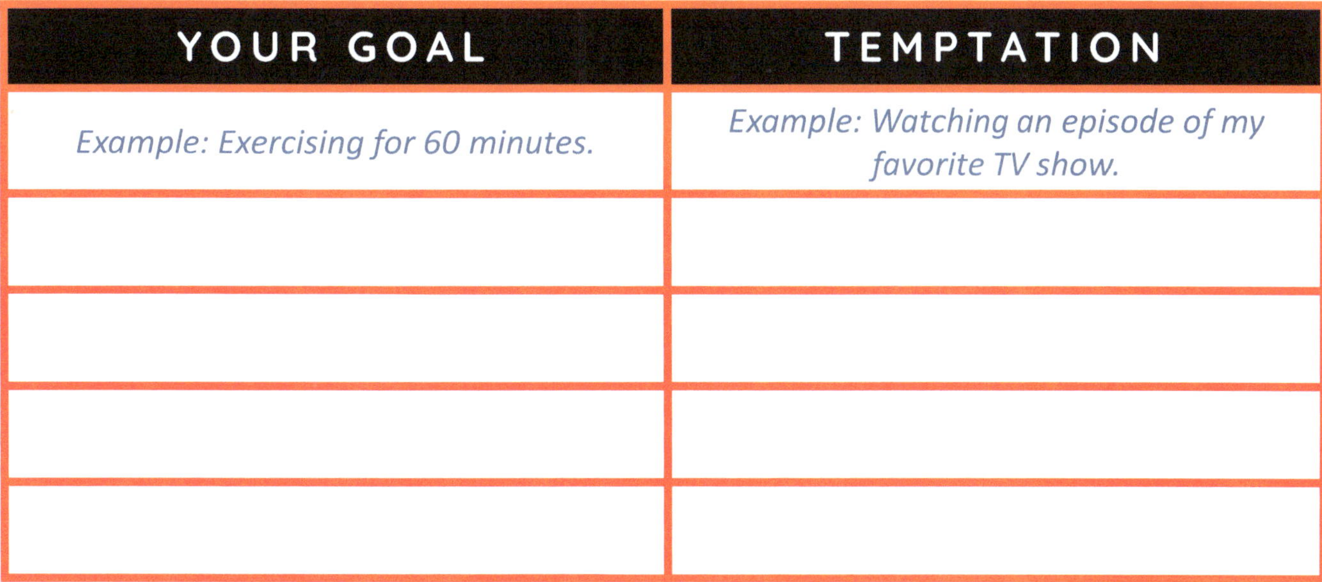

YOUR GOAL	TEMPTATION
Example: Exercising for 60 minutes.	*Example: Watching an episode of my favorite TV show.*

Note: Temptation bundling won't work well if you exercise for 60 minutes and then eat junk food. Research reveals it's important to ask yourself **WHY** you are doing what you are doing. This will motivate you to stay on track with or without temptation bundling! Also, make sure temptation bundling doesn't undermine your goals.

The Secret to Happiness
Is Gratefulness

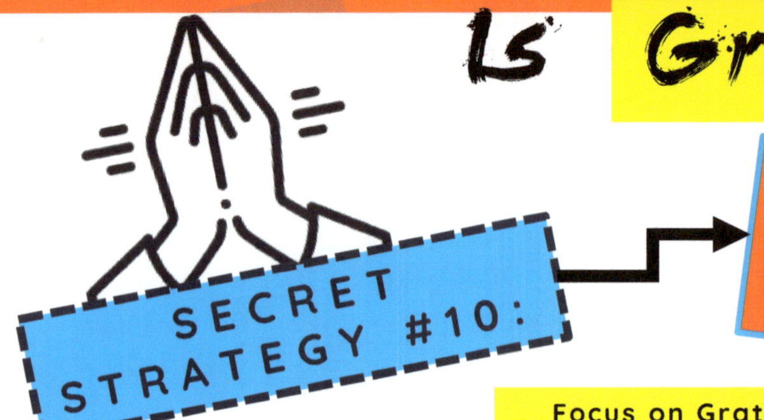

Having an "attitude of gratitude" can increase your oxytocin, serotonin, and dopamine levels. Grateful people report higher levels of life satisfaction and lower levels of depression and stress.

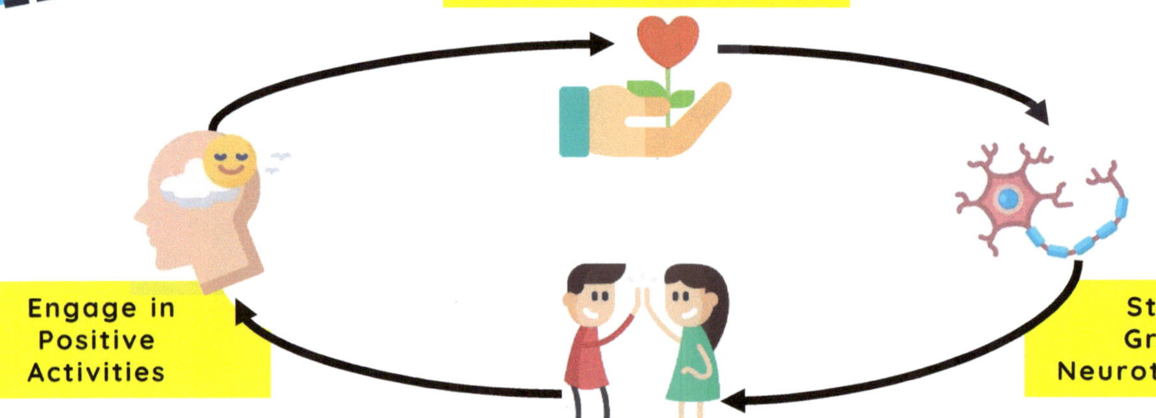

The saying "*Neurons that fire together, wire together*" means that when you help your brain activate oxytocin and serotonin through gratefulness, it will continue to seek and look for other ways to be grateful in your life. It's very common for humans to focus on the problems they are having or what's not going right in their lives. Unfortunately, this type of thinking naturally leads the brain to focus on negativity.

When we practice gratitude, we are able to activate our neurons in a positive way and focus on what's going right! This makes our neurons stronger, and the brain begins to actively look for other things to be grateful for.

Whatever we focus on grows. We can water either the weeds or the flowers in our minds. If we focus on the negative, our negative pathways grow and we begin to water and grow weeds. Thus, we are not happy and we constantly compare our lives to that of others. However, if we focus on the positive by practicing gratefulness, our positive pathways grow and we begin to water and grow beautiful flowers. This allows us to experience happiness with who we are and what we have in our lives. With a positive mindset, we have a happier outlook on life and can attract more positivity into our lives!

My **Gratitude** Journal

TAKE A WALK OUTSIDE
and write down some things
you are grateful for.

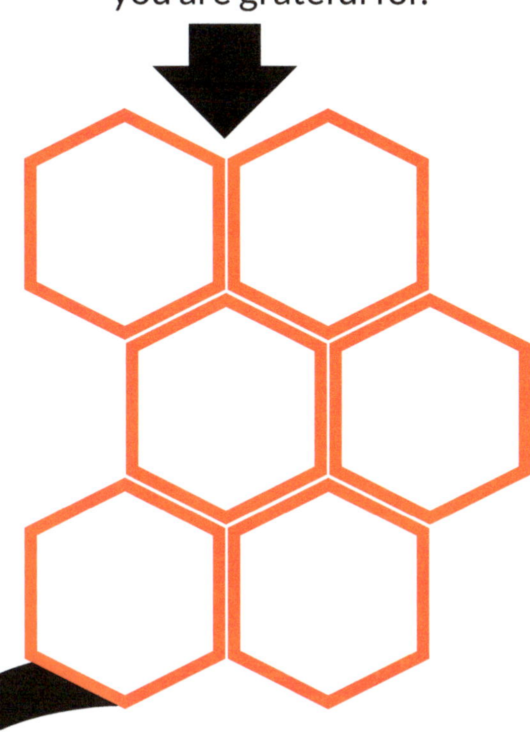

MENTALLY THANK SOMEONE that did something for you this week.

WHAT PLACES are you grateful to have in your life?

WHAT FOODS are you grateful to have in your life?

WHO are you grateful to have in your life?

What are 3 **THINGS** you are grateful for today?

1

2

3

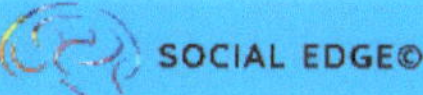

Co-Creating a Contract

This contract is being co-created by _______________ (*student*) and ___________________(*parent/teacher*).

	Goals/ Visualize Your Intentions	Rewards / Temptation Bundling
ACADEMIC	*I will [**what?**] at [**where?**] in [**when?**].*	After I _______________________ _______________________ I will get to _______________________ _______________________.
PERSONAL GROWTH	*I will [**what?**] at [**where?**] in [**when?**].*	After I _______________________ _______________________ I will get to _______________________ _______________________.
PASSION PROJECT (ONGOING TASKS)	*I will [**what?**] at [**where?**] in [**when?**].*	After Task 1 __________ is completed, I will get to _______________________. After the entire Passion Project is launched, I will get to _____________ _______________________.

COMMITMENT: We recognize that the rewards are a privilege for getting a goal accomplished. By signing this contract, we each commit to implementing the goals we set <u>before</u> we get the predetermined rewards.

I hereby commit to abiding by the rules set out in this agreement.

SIGNATURES:

parent(s) or teacher   student

DATE: